Lizzie Smith

Mermaid on Legs

Indigo Dreams Publishing

First Edition: Mermaid on Legs
First published in Great Britain in 2020 by:
Indigo Dreams Publishing
24, Forest Houses
Cookworthy Moor
Halwill
Beaworthy
Devon
EX21 5UU

www.indigodreams.co.uk

ISBN 978-1-912876-32-7

British Library Cataloguing in Publication Data. A CIP record for this book can be obtained from the British Library.

Designed and typeset in Palatino Linotype by Indigo Dreams.
Cover design by Ronnie Goodyer at Indigo Dreams
Printed and bound in Great Britain by 4edge Ltd.

Papers used by Indigo Dreams are recyclable products made from wood grown in sustainable forests following the guidance of the Forest Stewardship Council.

To my father
and poet, D.E. Poole

Acknowledgements

My thanks go to: Melinda Tetley for reading early manuscripts, FlyontheWall Press for allowing publication of *Shutting up Shop – Last Lay*, Helena Nelson for comments on four poems and Live Canon for feedback on the sestina.

Mermaid on Legs is Lizzie Smith's debut collection.

CONTENTS

Making Waves

Earthbound

Bust Up

Out, at sea

We are all terrestrial

Mermaid on Legs

Making Waves

Shape Shifter

I am one of the shoal of silver fish
that dart and swim in unison;
I am the wave that gathers speed and height
and crashes in a glorious foamy mess;
then I am strapped to the prow of a stormy ship
exposed to the elements, a vain mascot;
then I am cast in stone on a quay in Denmark
pawed over, snapped at, universally admired;
I am a seal who dives after supper
and enjoys a tasty morsel of squid;
I am the singer of songs near rocks,
warning you – too late I fear.
We are all bound to this universe
if not by time, by matter, I hear.

Under the Deep

From under the deep, the stars feel wet
like glowing jellyfish swimming above.
The twinkles sway, bobbing
like blobs, but untouchable.

Light filters down at night,
discos for dolphins are far away;
my cathedral is thronged by whales
baleening mournful lullabies.

Floating by on every side
are lightweight bottles without a message:
we'd like to throttle them
before they choke us, belly up.

Save the Mermaid

Mermaid, you dive into the
world-wide web of messages,

bobbing drunkenly on the tide.
then sucked back in, jetsamed,

you hold on for dear life
to weed that will save you.

Clinging, you drift near to shore
to spy the red lights of harbour.

Leery Len gives you a leg aboard,
bangs you till you've seen the fireworks.

Grateful he read your semaphore
you slip back into the ether.

You drown the sorrow of fishes
by entrancing screens

with your topless half:
submerging the alien bottom.

Your voice once rang out across the waves,
it now stutters in dashes and dots.

In the story the sisters salvage you
before you are scattered like frothy foam.

Angel Mermaids

Falling five fathoms
mermaids feel weightless,
even embracing
bodies of sailors.

Anchor tattoos plummet
down to the sea bed;
while angel mermaids
ascend, saving again.

Beach dancing

The music drew them into shore,
the silent sirens wondered
at the Dionysian dancers
making a spectacle.

Potbellies gyrating in the waves
Maenad naiads untressed,
but what a Bacchanalian beat
to set tails a-twitch, bewitch.

And so the beery lads and babes
not quite knowing what they'd imbibed
danced in the waves with mermaids
completing the Cycladean circle.

One-night stand

The boat had been anchored close to shore
for three days or more. I crept close
to peek through portholes and saw a
solitary seaman left to guard the ship.

He started to enjoy the freedom to take a dip
and strip he did. I swam under
to nudge him with my tail. When he dived,
I wrapped my hair around his neck.

His eyes met mine under green water,
spluttering we surfaced, curious.
I smelt his sweat and fingered his golden chest:
he grasped my arm to gaze upon me.

Half staggering he carried me to a cove
covert behind a curtain of weed, to bed.
Writhing, we tentacled our way to pleasure,
salty kisses, slipping between embraces.

I was no small beer or dry biscuit,
no measly measure of rum for the thirsty.
I was a fleshy fish toasted, warm,
a skinful of full-bodied wine.

I did not come to torment men in storms
with dark thoughts of losing home and love;
I came in the broad light of day,
to dalliance, to board my sailor boy.

How do you mount a mermaid?

How do you mount a mermaid?
That's the question on everyone's lips,
That's the eternal mystery –
not whether they really exist.

Well, have you heard of a mermaid's purse?
On shore it's crackly and dry;
immersed, it's wet and makes a pocket
to wriggle a finger in and pry.

Use your imagination, then,
to work out how to grapple,
bed her on the rocking wave –
without gulping too much water.

Footless

There again maybe it's a bondage thing?
I've no legs to run away from you,
just a tail to flick if I'm not on land,
stuck with a lame duck of a sailor.

Landed, I'm like a fish out of water,
gasping – not with desire, you ninny.
It's not my way to thrash about girlishly,
only when I'm slipping out of your grip –

Leglass

Smashed at a party on a beach,
you lay neck up
bottom exposed
left to greet the morning rays on your own.
The incoming tide caressed and
enfolded you in its breasting wave,
danced you around,
worked its relentless magic,
took off those rough edges,
tide after tide
cast you up again for collection,
still beautiful, with light shining through:
sea glass.

Mermaid Girl

She thought it would be easy to walk
upright through the human maze
of love affairs and court politics,
when she surfaced, came to land.

She put one foot in front of the
other and wore her bravest smile;
but underneath those fishnet tights
pain seared through her pelvis.

Knives she felt garrotting her groin,
and flash in the eyes of sycophants.
She'd given up her only weapon:
her sweet voice that could charm men.

She danced the dance of the seven veils
fluid, supple, supplicant.
While, hanging on his every word,
fawned the silken sherbet harem.

She'd forfeited her gang of girls
to pursue this dream of a Prince.
Were earth maids born to suffer this?
Who wanted little mermaids?

Mermaid Undone

He loves me not.
The petal drops.
I wilt and droop,
cling to the galleon's rail.

Will what the witch foretold
come full true? Ah –
I look my last at the sky
running red, streaking

down. I stream into
the sea, salty sick
to the stomach at losing to Her.
Your limpid brown eyes

imprinted on me, fade
as I return to the wave
that bore me. Torn up
I become frothy foam.

I'm in my element
riding high, low,
joined by wraiths, maids
sundered; rising again.

Earthbound

Selkie

She chose him:
disentangled herself
from her angel element
of underworld seaweed

and ascended to join him
in his manly realm
of smelly diesel fumes
and fisher oilskins.

His anchor-tattooed biceps
pulled her aboard,
caught her, clasped her,
his scratchy beard like sand.

She entered his house
and lay down in his bed,
rose up in the morning
and did as a wife.

Caul again

"Open your legs!" you call.
Standing in the swimming pool,
I play the entrance gate
for you to swim under.

Forcing your way through,
you bump me as you did in labour.
Strange to feel your wet hair
and insistent push again.

Foal-like, second thrust you were
through, long legs and all,
burst free from the confining womb,
your private swimming pool.

It had been underwater,
umbilical, gill heaven,
endless back flips, diving,
cheeky somersaults and turns.

Into the world you tumbled,
into a bath you swam with joy,
with a cap of waters on your head,
my little water-bearing Aquarian.

A Tale of Five Ewes

The first sheep was penned in stocks,
her head sticking through a hole,
hindquarters exposed to the
onslaught of the desperate lamb.

She kicked, lashed out
at being asked to mother another's.
The lamb was hungry; she was angry
at the universe for confining her so.

The second ewe was dejected,
in pain at losing hers and getting infected.
She huddled back, the orphan was rejected:
she wasn't in the mood to mother any others.

The third ewe was being presented
with a lamb in lamb's clothing,
the skinned fleece smelling of another,
to try and trick a new mother.

Twins nestled yin and yang in a bucket,
their Mum had had them premature,
but her milk didn't come in. Stunned,
she shuffled off and left them cold.

The farmer's grandson, all of six,
scooped them up, to warm under a lamp.
That's what happened to our twins
looking wide-eyed at them now.

Mothering is like that. Half your
Offspring's blood is not your own,
your baby an alien mouth that sucks
and screams and there's no space for you.

You sidle to the other side of the room
in post-partum pain, feel trapped.
It takes time to bond, to grow
into the sheepskin of motherhood.

Puffling

Jester, you bob on the waves spraying hilarity
as you beak jokes with your sister.

Harlequin, you strut your stuff
atop rocks, but only in the family circle.

Flapper, sometimes it gets too much
and your wings beat double-breasted time.

Burrower, cheek at my chest, you find
soft sanctuary from the circling gulls.

Dancer, you slid in and out of my dreams
till you took your bow on the Isle of May.

Diver before you could swim, you slipped
into the water – surfacing again on the horizon.

Survivor of being on the red list
and coasting many a swell,

Faithful, you return time after time
to give your Ma a peck – my little puffin.

The Migraine

That hammerhead of a shark
has swooped down, to eat up peace
of head and happiness;
drain the sea of wet fish.

He comes pounding left temple,
left temple, blinding with pain,
throwing his cape of darkness
on a world of light and vision.

He sends shivers down under,
turns bowels to water,
reduces you to a jellyfish
craving cave cover.

He ruins birthday parties,
trashes whole days of life.
turn to face him: he's just
a gape of appetite.

Winter Welkin Keening

Where can you find me when winter winds whistle?
under the welkin, white with frost,
on a calm day when low tides plash,
and blue hills fade to vanishing point.

In the biting breezes of the North,
I bulk up blubber in defence, and lie
with my sisters, far away from you,
flapping my flippers to keep circulation.

Nipples unsucked by searching mouths
hibernate and hope for warmer dawns,
where engine oil is not pumped out
and swallowed up by wide-eyed pups.

On a dry night, when you're in bed
we rise for moon rites – and dance
round bonfires in a banshee frenzy
keening for a return to selkie sanity.

Sea Weeds

From the kist they murmur to me,
with the incoming sea, the surging tide.

For many a year they've lain there, dormant,
while babies dozed and sucked on me, till I was dry.

Moonlight falls. Alone in the room I take them out
to try on: parchment crisp, but still sea tight.

Dare I leave the babes awhile for a quick dip,
to test them out, my flipper-flappers?

That night I deigned to enter his bed, I hid my pass
to the underworld, so I could return.

My breasts brace the crashing waves, salt's up my nose,
pure sinew joy of bucking surge and tail.

I'd forgotten the adrenaline rush, the need for speed,
the slide of water on skin and scale, the cleansing –

swimming in my element, free as a mermaid.

Bust Up

The Tenth Day

It has been searingly hot for the tenth day,
my skin is shrivelling, itching to be cast off,
like a snake, like the chameleon I am.

I long to immerse myself, like a babe
in the waters and be reborn, reborne
on the waves, pickled in salt like a herring.

But here I sit outside my husband's hut,
staring out to the sea to the horizon, and down
at my feet on the marble flagstones.

If I give him a cup more wine, and a tickle,
perhaps he'll slumber deep and I'll creep
down to the shore and away.

Mélissande

If there's one thing that slays me,
It's the timbre of a voice,
sonorous and low, singing to me
tales of the sea and faraway kingdoms.
And so you captivated me,
Mélissande, on a sandy beach
in Spain, in a bar by the sea,
over a salty sundowner.
Seven sweet years you gave me, on
and off as I came ashore.
Children four you bore,
and here they are, strong and fair.
Now you're gone out to sea I stare
and wonder if you are there.

Water Sources

When I'm lubbed on land, I gasp for water
but on this Mediterranean desert island
there's none – or precious little – to go around.

Giorgos had the source of the spring;
I got a trickle below, only in winter.
So I sneaked up a hose, for a supply.

World war three broke out and I retired
back to the salty sea –
as I do not have to live on fresh water.

Proud

Like a witch they tried
to duck and drown,
she bobs to the surface,
borne up by billowing skirts,
her hair a halo of seaweed.

The recurring nightmare
of her resurfacing skeleton
taunts the tormentors
as she becomes sanctified
in body, by the water.

Like the figurehead maid displayed
on the jutting battleship Unicorn,
chest first, breast exposed, unfurled,
she will not be cowed:
she rises proud.

Mermaid Attack

Splayed on the surface she lay
lashed to flotsam:
lacerated by wind,
bound by slimy seaweed.

To the heavens she fixed her eye,
trusting the North Star to guide her way.
Those folk from below were tugging her down,
pulling at her gown, picking away,

trying their mightiest to undo the ballast
of her main, but in vain:
for the heat of the midday sun
shrivelled them all up.

Out, At Sea

Chain Maid

Neptune knows how long I've been anchored
in this muddy sand, somnambulant,
moved back and forth by bobbing tide,
out and in, then flung upside down.

I'm tugged awake by the tanker setting off
dragging me behind in its wake.
Like a great umbilical chain it keeps
me on a leash, at a distance.

When the ship pauses I can dive
and play like a dog on a long lead,
sniffing the salt, licking my lips,
letting the water slip over my back.

The game of tethering soon wearies though,
I am a seamaid, used to roaming wide.
The chain rattles like an ankle shackle,
I strain to be free again.

I wake, moored in a New World harbour,
to towering blocks for blokes insuring ships,
windows peering down at a freak of nature.
Consigned as a creature, I stare at the circus.

Unlabelled

Glass jars of specimens are lined in rows
cheek to jowl with stuffed dead parrots.

We examine the long nose of a shrew floating,
a foetus, not in amniotic fluid.

Baby marsupials pinched from pouches
by overzealous Victorian scientists

stand catalogued and clinical;
but, for the mother, there was blood and goo.

How many nameless girls now squat in loos
producing hot, soft mini-versions?

Sister Snail

He used to –
when we used to –
tie up plants
sort things out.

The snail makes slow progress
up the daisy stalk
putting out her little feelers
as if to talk.

I'd like to say to her –
she said rashly to me –
let's get together
lock horns and have it out.

Senior Mermaids

Old Mermaids have wrinkles too, you know
a sign of seniority, wisdom, stripes earned
in salty sun, guarding wrecked survivors –
or scolding silly little mermaids sporting.

They can be so cheeky it makes me want to
cut out their wagging tongues, but I'm no witch.
I treasure their lulling voices in sunset songs
and marvel at their slick flicks in unison.

My wrinkly dugs hang down: they've given suck
to sweet lips of swimmers limpetted on,
who grew to darting minnows hide-and-seeking
till they left for far-off treasure shores.

My tail has lost its sparkly sequin sheen –
now replaced by decorative hangers on,
who cling to me to show my queenly status.
Necklaces nestle and gleam in my grooves.

Now I wait for the dolphin time, to rise
to the surface to coast again, holding fins,
feeling the speed I've lost. Then sink,
thankfully, for quiet drinks with the old men.

Mermaid Cruising

I've been out here aeons now
you might think I'd grace a prow:
bust thrust up, tail merged in,
but I'm half submerged, dandering,

dillying, shilly-shallying
in the shallows, lady-in-waiting
for men to hearken to me –
I'm not just a siren of the sea.

It's rare that boats with lads pass,
no time to look for a lass –
all eyes are fixed to the screen –
the stars, the sights unseen.

Only old boys on a cruise,
in wheelchairs, get to enthuse
and to the bar attendants rave:
I swear, I saw a mermaid wave.

Selkie Sestina

Where man does not see, the sea
parts itself to let out a mermaid
who seeks to bathe in sun or moonlight,
making the mirror a prop on her stage.
The backdrop depicts a porpoise rise
and sink, into the middle-distance.

And well she might want to keep her distance:
flotsam and jetsam on the sea
has seen an unholy rise
encroaching on the world of mermaid
till it's even got to the stage
of blocking out her heavenly light.

And she had thought shafts of light
would never be made foggy in the distance,
by soggy plastics in their last stage
of breakdown. You'd refuse to use the sea
as anything other than the refuge of mermaids –
and gulping fish who come to rise

and take the air. To think the rise
of man has come to take so light
the rights of water-dwelling mermaids!
Have we really come a distance
from clam-eating cave-dwellers by the sea
who observed the season and marked the stage

and progress of planets? Who at every stage
rejoiced in the warmth of a sun's rise,
believed in spirits coming out of the seas,
longed to submerse themselves with delight –
did not want to keep their distance –
to stroke a selkie, meld with a mermaid.

Now only satellites spot mermaids.
Men strut on a virtual stage,
relationships are invariably long distance;
discarded bits and bobs are on the rise.
Will they never see the light?
For behind the screen is a salty sea.

The future's not distant. There's a mermaid.
The sea's a stage that tells a tale of the rise
and dimming of night's light.

Her Last Will

I give my body to:
Sandy.
May my hair mat like ropes of seaweed
my heart slip out like a dead electric jellyfish
my skull bleach like coral bones
my skin flake like rainbow trout scales
my waist waste into morning fog
my teeth be mistaken for shells
and adorn a child's fantasy of a castle:
May I be reborn as Joy.
dust to dust
sand to sand
mer to mer.

We Are All Terrestrial

Sea Trove

The twinkle of speckles of sand,
cascading in the sunlit wave,
a pearl inside a nacred shell,
the diamonds of salt between rocks,
silver moonlight playing,
the antique piles of rocks
secreting ancient ammonites,
cowrie shells used as coin,
the abounding blue gold of water,
the harnessing of the Zephyr breeze
and the towering tidal wave –
from the ebony boom of thunder
to the most intricate seahorse:
these are the treasures of my kingdom.

John the Baptist and the bees

Freeze frames, snapshots of the man:
leaping in Elizabeth's womb on meeting Mary;
wild man of the desert eating locusts and honey;
his head on a platter, offered at Herod's feast.

So he's frozen in time by the records of him,
no sense of the prophet's pronouncements in between.
But on withdrawing his drawer from the hive
we see the bees crawling like marks on the page:

The buzz of his angry words come down to us,
even if they're climbing all over each other, jumbled;
unlike the neat Gospel of John with a static
painting of John the Baptist christening Christ.

Bees Wax Lyrical

The bees sizzle,
crawling and slipping
in their haste
to evade observation
of the veiled keeper.

"DO NOT DISTURB
was posted at the gate,
didn't you see?"
they hum angrily,
mumble resentfully.

"We've been managing fine
for millennia you know,
John the Baptist bear
plunged in his dirty great paw,
long ago now.

Virgil wrote his Georgics
extolling our nurses,
praising our queens,
despising our drones –
the buzz is not that bad is it?

Well you nasty crew
with chemical warfare
on our noble race:
we've got a sting in our tail
to use as a last resort."

Snowdrops

First to burst on the scene are
pretty, hardy snowdrops, shy, yet
bursting with pride at being the first
to put on their costumes, heralding Spring.

The Hunter

My father used to hunt the first primrose
of spring, with a lightness in his step,
and I follow his footsteps searching you
my tiny Giant Snowdrop, hiding your face.

Seeking where you appeared last year,
I find my girls spotted you before me,
narrowly avoiding you, when they jumped
off their trampoline with a burst.

I turn you upside down just to check
as the midwife does – boy or girl?
Your bits are tucked up, neatly formed,
with a streak of yellow in the mix.

I think again what it might have been like
to have had that experience,
but none of the green shoots in my grass
were to be made with trumpets drooping down.

White jewels now pop out on my lawn,
like the constellation of The Hunter.
I bend to greet the new generation
and pick just three to sniff and remember.

Messenger

Sometime, one time, you were treading the earth
until you slipped off this spinning planet.
I still feel that I might walk into you:
one day turn the corner and bump into you.

How odd that you talked politics, lay on your
back to admire the stars, stood on your head,
believed you were Mercury the messenger,
then posted yourself off to another world –
without leaving a note or mark behind.

Epiphany 2019
On the discovery of Ultimate Thule

Will snowmen melt out of existence
and be remembered in folklore
as being as rare as White Christmases
or lakes freezing over?

I stare at the new 'snowman'
the paper says has been discovered –
seeing the sign of infinity
as a kind of Trump balloon.

Now we gods do not follow the stars,
we mount and ride past them.
Where are the wise men and women
to halt this flat earth slide?

Naiads and Dryads have been boxed out

One by one
each shade expires,
goes Hades-ward:
Naiads and Dryads have
been boxed out
subterraneaned
by concrete.

They rise up trying to escape,
but finding no worshippers
(they're all in pine-fragranced spas)
they sink, soft and sad
back into Ea the earth.

Their mother's arms
enfold them tight,
so they can't slip
up to the weary world
of stinking fumes
and rotting garbage
and foul-mouthed men.

She knows but can't tell them that
since Greek triangulation
and New Town saturation
to resist is
strangulation of oneself
with planners' red tape.

In Limbo they dream of steaming glades –
of riding rivulets –
of embracing and faining to embrace.
Hooded, they wait the day
that they will be resurrected;
and men plunged into shade.

What the Mermaid saw

Under the deep, blue sea,
what should the mermaid see
caught in the waving weed?

Jellyfish-hanging string:
a castaway tampon.
(she can't do much with it.)

Seahorses riding on
steeds made of weird earbuds,
entangled, shackled down.

There's an unsheathed razor
(past nicking razorbills)
Razor shells hate its cheek.

Slicker than quiff of hair,
gobs come, of oil spewed out
bills of gulls, their calls choked.

Scrabbling no more, a seal
sporting a necklace net:
glazed over big, doe eyes.

Muzzled by plastic ring
greatest of beasts laid low,
sea lion casts his crown.

In the kingdom above,
their view's obscured by screens,
as all asphyxiate.

Shutting up Shop: Last Lay

And the sedge warbler shut up her basket shop
down by the river,
along with the lapwing who had lost her field nest
to the tractors again,
and the corncrake croaked her last.

And the village barber moved to the city mall.

And the puffin skidded onto his home rockface
faint with hunger – and expired
from lack of eels swimming in the warm seas.

*And the monger of fish was swallowed whole by a whale of a Super
Market franchise.*

And the microbeads adorned the oysters and choked their pearls.

*And the Finisterre radio waves dried up –
only octogenarians were listening: a marginal audience of a
million is easily jetsamed.*

And the Totten Galcier melted to become a tottering heap
of snow and water crying snowmen's tears into the salty sea.

*And another child's little lungs collapsed:
choked from the fumes of a million cars
and Bangkok tuk-tuks stuck in traffic jams.*

And the hedgehog landed on its back, feet kicking in the air,
in his last attempt to cross the carriageway to Mrs Tiddleywink:
no longer trampled by hooves of horses;
but squeezed out of invention by Motor Cars and Jeeps.

And the greengrocer failed to support its market gardeners:
no more knobbly carrots and weird phallic shapes
or potatoes with beautiful heart-shaped bottoms.

And the morning chorus became muted.
Every spring the voices thinned until
the voice of the turtle dove was heard no more in our land;
only the call of ravens sounded the knell of nature –
should anyone have been listening with their earphones out.

And so the lights in the High Street went out one by one
until the offshore lot had made a desert of the heart of our community.

And the voice of the turtle dove was heard no more in our land.

Urgent

DAISY ██████ NOT ME HIVE DIVE TORMENTIL

FORGET ██████ BOG COTTON BOG ASPHODEL BOG

████ ME IN ███ CLOVE R AGWORT RAGGED ROBIN

BUTTERCUP STOP SPOT TED ORCHID

NO LADY'S SMOCK ██████ ME NOT POLLINATE

SWEET VIOLET NOT VIOLATE SELF HEAL

DENT-DE-LION ██████ ME NOT NOTE

GRASS OF PARNASSUS FORGET ██████ FORGOTTEN

VIPER'S BUG LOSS ███████ NOT KNOTWEED

EYEBRIGHT NO A NO BEE NO C

FORGET ██████ VETCH BIRD'S FOOT TREFOIL

ST JOHNS WORT, SNEEZEWORT, FORGET ME ████

THRIFT, THISTLE THY ██████ ME ███ ZZZ

YARROW, BLUEBELL MEADOWSWEET ████ ME ███ HUM

FORGET ME NOT ███ TANT ███ TINCT XX

Indigo Dreams Publishing Ltd
24, Forest Houses
Cookworthy Moor
Halwill
Beaworthy
Devon
EX21 5UU
www.indigodreams.co.uk